$2199
5

# SYMPHONIES
## Nos. 8 and 9 ("New World")
### IN FULL SCORE

# Antonín Dvořák

Dover Publications, Inc.
New York

The publisher is grateful to The George Sherman Dickinson Music Library, Vassar College, for lending its copy of Symphony No. 8 for photographing; and to the Sibley Music Library, Eastman School of Music, University of Rochester, for lending its copy of Symphony No. 9.

Published in Canada by General Publishing Company, Ltd., 30 Lesmill Road, Don Mills, Toronto, Ontario.
Published in the United Kingdom by Constable and Company, Ltd.

This Dover edition, first published in 1984, is an unabridged and unaltered republication of *Symphony (No. 4) in G Major*, originally published by Novello and Company, Limited, London, in 1892, and *Aus der neuen Welt. "Z nového světa." Symphonie (No. 5, E moll.) für grosses Orchester, Op. 95. Partitur*, originally published by N. Simrock, Berlin, in 1894.

Manufactured in the United States of America
Dover Publications, Inc., 31 East 2nd Street, Mineola, N.Y. 11501

**Library of Congress Cataloging in Publications Data**

Dvořák, Antonín, 1841–1904.
  Symphonies nos. 8 and 9.

  Reprint (1st work). Originally published: London : Novello, 1892.
  Reprint (2nd work). Originally published: Berlin : Simrock, 1894.
  1. Symphonies—Scores.  I. Dvořák, Antonin, 1841–1904.  Symphonies, no. 9, op. 95, E minor.  1984.
M1001.D97  no. 8  1984                    84-5012
ISBN 0-486-24749-X

# Contents

# Symphony No. 8
## in G Major, Op. 88

# I.

Change to Flauto II.

# II.

# III.

CODA.

# IV.

# Symphony No. 9 ("New World")
## in E Minor, Op. 95

# II.

# III. Scherzo.

# IV.

# *Dover Piano and Keyboard Editions*

**THE WELL-TEMPERED CLAVIER: Books I and II, Complete, Johann Sebastian Bach.** All 48 preludes and fugues in all major and minor keys. Authoritative Bach-Gesellschaft edition. Explanation of ornaments in English, tempo indications, music corrections. 208pp. 9⅜ × 12¼.
24532-2 Pa. **$9.95**

**KEYBOARD MUSIC, J. S. Bach.** Bach-Gesellschaft edition. For harpsichord, piano, other keyboard instruments. English Suites, French Suites, Six Partitas, Goldberg Variations, Two-Part Inventions, Three-Part Sinfonias. 312pp. 8⅛ × 11. 22360-4 Pa. **$12.95**

**ITALIAN CONCERTO, CHROMATIC FANTASIA AND FUGUE AND OTHER WORKS FOR KEYBOARD, Johann Sebastian Bach.** Sixteen of Bach's best-known, most-performed and most-recorded works for the keyboard, reproduced from the authoritative Bach-Gesellschaft edition. 112pp. 9 × 12. 25387-2 Pa. **$8.95**

**COMPLETE KEYBOARD TRANSCRIPTIONS OF CONCERTOS BY BAROQUE COMPOSERS, Johann Sebastian Bach.** Sixteen concertos by Vivaldi, Telemann and others, transcribed for solo keyboard instruments. Bach-Gesellschaft edition. 128pp. 9⅜ × 12¼.
25529-8 Pa. **$9.95**

**ORGAN MUSIC, J. S. Bach.** Bach-Gesellschaft edition. 93 works. 6 Trio Sonatas, German Organ Mass, Orgelbüchlein, Six Schubler Chorales, 18 Choral Preludes. 357pp. 8⅛ × 11. 22359-0 Pa. **$13.95**

**COMPLETE PRELUDES AND FUGUES FOR ORGAN, Johann Sebastian Bach.** All 25 of Bach's complete sets of preludes and fugues (i.e. compositions written as pairs), from the authoritative Bach-Gesellschaft edition. 168pp. 8⅜ × 11. 24816-X Pa. **$10.95**

**TOCCATAS, FANTASIAS, PASSACAGLIA AND OTHER WORKS FOR ORGAN, J. S. Bach.** Over 20 best-loved works including Toccata and Fugue in D Minor, BWV 565; Passacaglia and Fugue in C Minor, BWV 582, many more. Bach-Gesellschaft edition. 176pp. 9 × 12.
25403-8 Pa. **$10.95**

**TWO- AND THREE-PART INVENTIONS, J. S. Bach.** Reproduction of original autograph ms. Edited by Eric Simon. 62pp. 8⅛ × 11.
21982-8 Pa. **$8.95**

**THE 36 FANTASIAS FOR KEYBOARD, Georg Philipp Telemann.** Graceful compositions by 18th-century master. 1923 Breslauer edition. 80pp. 8⅛ × 11. 25365-1 Pa. **$6.95**

**GREAT KEYBOARD SONATAS, Carl Philipp Emanuel Bach.** Comprehensive two-volume edition contains 51 sonatas by second, most important son of Johann Sebastian Bach. Originality, rich harmony, delicate workmanship. Authoritative French edition. Total of 384pp. 8⅜ × 11¼.
Series I 24853-4 Pa. **$11.95**
Series II 24854-2 Pa. **$10.95**

**KEYBOARD WORKS/Series One: Ordres I–XIII; Series Two: Ordres XIV–XXVII and Miscellaneous Pieces, François Couperin.** Over 200 pieces. Reproduced directly from edition prepared by Johannes Brahms and Friedrich Chrysander. Total of 496pp. 8⅛ × 11.
Series I 25795-9 Pa. **$10.95**
Series II 25796-7 Pa. **$11.95**

**KEYBOARD WORKS FOR SOLO INSTRUMENTS, G. F. Handel.** 35 neglected works from Handel's vast oeuvre, originally jotted down as improvisations. Includes Eight Great Suites, others. New sequence. 174pp. 9⅜ × 12¼. 24338-9 Pa. **$10.95**

**WORKS FOR ORGAN AND KEYBOARD, Jan Pieterszoon Sweelinck.** Nearly all of early Dutch composer's difficult-to-find keyboard works. Chorale variations; toccatas, fantasias; variations on secular, dance tunes. Also, incomplete and/or modified works, plus fantasia by John Bull. 272pp. 9 × 12. 24935-2 Pa. **$14.95**

**ORGAN WORKS, Dietrich Buxtehude.** Complete organ works of extremely influential pre-Bach composer. Toccatas, preludes, chorales, more. Definitive Breitkopf & Härtel edition. 320pp. 8⅜ × 11¼. (Available in U.S. only) 25682-0 Pa. **$14.95**

**THE FUGUES ON THE MAGNIFICAT FOR ORGAN OR KEYBOARD, Johann Pachelbel.** 94 pieces representative of Pachelbel's magnificent contribution to keyboard composition; can be played on the organ, harpsichord or piano. 100pp. 9 × 12. (Available in U.S. only)
25037-7 Pa. **$8.95**

**MY LADY NEVELLS BOOKE OF VIRGINAL MUSIC, William Byrd.** 42 compositions in modern notation from 1591 ms. For any keyboard instrument. 245pp. 8⅛ × 11. 22246-2 Pa. **$13.95**

**ELIZABETH ROGERS HIR VIRGINALL BOOKE, edited with calligraphy by Charles J. F. Cofone.** All 112 pieces from noted 1656 manuscript, most never before published. Composers include Thomas Brewer, William Byrd, Orlando Gibbons, etc. 125pp. 9 × 12. 23138-0 Pa. **$10.95**

**THE FITZWILLIAM VIRGINAL BOOK, edited by J. Fuller Maitland, W. B. Squire.** Famous early 17th-century collection of keyboard music, 300 works by Morley, Byrd, Bull, Gibbons, etc. Modern notation. Total of 938pp. 8⅜ × 11. Two-vol. set. 21068-5, 21069-3 Pa. **$34.90**

**GREAT KEYBOARD SONATAS, Series I and Series II, Domenico Scarlatti.** 78 of the most popular sonatas reproduced from the G. Ricordi edition edited by Alessandro Longo. Total of 320pp. 8⅛ × 11¼.
Series I 24996-4 Pa. **$9.95**
Series II 25003-2 Pa. **$9.95**

**COMPLETE PIANO SONATAS, Joseph Haydn.** 52 sonatas reprinted from authoritative Breitkopf & Härtel edition. Extremely clear and readable; ample space for notes, analysis. 464pp. 9⅜ × 12¼. 24726-0 Pa. **$11.95**
24727-9 Pa. **$11.95**

**BAGATELLES, RONDOS AND OTHER SHORTER WORKS FOR PIANO, Ludwig van Beethoven.** Most popular and most performed shorter works, including Rondo a capriccio in G and Andante in F. Breitkopf & Härtel edition. 128pp. 9⅜ × 12¼. 25392-9 Pa. **$8.95**

**COMPLETE VARIATIONS FOR SOLO PIANO, Ludwig van Beethoven.** Contains all 21 sets of Beethoven's piano variations, including the extremely popular *Diabelli Variations, Op. 120.* 240pp. 9⅜ × 12¼.
25188-8 Pa. **$12.95**

**COMPLETE PIANO SONATAS, Ludwig van Beethoven.** All sonatas in fine Schenker edition, with fingering, analytical material. One of best modern editions. 615pp. 9 × 12. Two-vol. set. 23134-8, 23135-6 Pa. **$25.90**

**COMPLETE SONATAS FOR PIANOFORTE SOLO, Franz Schubert.** All 15 sonatas. Breitkopf and Härtel edition. 293pp. 9⅜ × 12¼.
22647-6 Pa. **$13.95**

**DANCES FOR SOLO PIANO, Franz Schubert.** Over 350 waltzes, minuets, landler, ecossaises, other charming, melodic dance compositions reprinted from the authoritative Breitkopf & Härtel edition. 192pp. 9⅜ × 12¼.
26107-7 Pa. **$11.95**

*Available from your music dealer or write for **free** Music Catalog to*
*Dover Publications, Inc., Dept. MUBI, 31 East 2nd Street, Mineola, N.Y. 11501.*

# Dover Piano and Keyboard Editions

**ORGAN WORKS, César Franck.** Composer's best-known works for organ, including Six Pieces, Trois Pieces, and Trois Chorals. Oblong format for easy use at keyboard. Authoritative Durand edition. 208pp. 11⅜ × 8¼.
25517-4 Pa. **$13.95**

**IBERIA AND ESPAÑA: Two Complete Works for Solo Piano, Isaac Albeniz.** Spanish composer's greatest piano works in authoritative editions. Includes the popular "Tango." 192pp. 9 × 12.
25367-8 Pa. **$10.95**

**GOYESCAS, SPANISH DANCES AND OTHER WORKS FOR SOLO PIANO, Enrique Granados.** Great Spanish composer's most admired, most performed suites for the piano, in definitive Spanish editions. 176pp. 9 × 12.
25481-X Pa. **$9.95**

**SELECTED PIANO COMPOSITIONS, César Franck, edited by Vincent d'Indy.** Outstanding selection of influential French composer's piano works, including early pieces and the two masterpieces—Prelude, Choral and Fugue; and Prelude, Aria and Finale. Ten works in all. 138pp. 9 × 12.
23269-7 Pa. **$10.95**

**THE COMPLETE PRELUDES AND ETUDES FOR PIANOFORTE SOLO, Alexander Scriabin.** All the preludes and etudes including many perfectly spun miniatures. Edited by K. N. Igumnov and Y. I. Mil'shteyn. 250pp. 9 × 12.
22919-X Pa. **$11.95**

**COMPLETE PIANO SONATAS, Alexander Scriabin.** All ten of Scriabin's sonatas, reprinted from an authoritative early Russian edition. 256pp. 8⅜ × 11¼.
25850-5 Pa. **$12.95**

**COMPLETE PRELUDES AND ETUDES-TABLEAUX, Serge Rachmaninoff.** Forty-one of his greatest works for solo piano, including the riveting C Minor, G-Minor and B-Minor preludes, in authoritative editions. 208pp. 8⅜ × 11¼.
25696-0 Pa. **$11.95**

**COMPLETE PIANO SONATAS, Sergei Prokofiev.** Definitive Russian edition of nine sonatas (1907–1953), among the most important compositions in the modern piano repertoire. 288pp. 8⅜ × 11¼. (Available in U.S. only)
25689-8 Pa. **$12.95**

**GYMNOPÉDIES, GNOSSIENNES AND OTHER WORKS FOR PIANO, Erik Satie.** The largest Satie collection of piano works yet published, 17 in all, reprinted from the original French editions. 176pp. 9 × 12. (Not available in France or Germany)
25978-1 Pa. **$10.95**

**TWENTY SHORT PIECES FOR PIANO (Sports et Divertissements), Erik Satie.** French master's brilliant thumbnail sketches—verbal and musical—of various outdoor sports and amusements. English translations, 20 illustrations. Rare, limited 1925 edition. 48pp. 12 × 8⅞. (Not available in France or Germany)
24365-6 Pa. **$6.95**

**COMPLETE PRELUDES, IMPROMPTUS AND VALSES-CAPRICES, Gabriel Fauré.** Eighteen elegantly wrought piano works in authoritative editions. Only one-volume collection. 144pp. 9 × 12. (Not available in France or Germany)
25789-4 Pa. **$8.95**

**PIANO MUSIC OF BÉLA BARTÓK, Series I, Béla Bartók.** New, definitive Archive Edition incorporating composer's corrections. Includes *Funeral March* from *Kossuth, Fourteen Bagatelles,* Bartók's break to modernism. 167pp. 9 × 12. (Available in U.S. only)
24108-4 Pa. **$11.95**

**PIANO MUSIC OF BÉLA BARTÓK, Series II, Béla Bartók.** Second in the Archive Edition incorporating composer's corrections. 85 short pieces *For Children, Two Elegies, Two Romanian Dances,* etc. 192pp. 9 × 12. (Available in U.S. only)
24109-2 Pa. **$11.95**

**FRENCH PIANO MUSIC, AN ANTHOLOGY, Isidor Phillipp (ed.).** 44 complete works, 1670–1905, by Lully, Couperin, Rameau, Alkan, Saint-Saëns, Delibes, Bizet, Godard, many others; favorites, lesser-known examples, but all top quality. 188pp. 9 × 12. (Not available in France or Germany)
23381-2 Pa. **$12.95**

**NINETEENTH-CENTURY EUROPEAN PIANO MUSIC: Unfamiliar Masterworks, John Gillespie (ed.).** Difficult-to-find etudes, toccatas, polkas, impromptus, waltzes, etc., by Albéniz, Bizet, Chabrier, Fauré, Smetana, Richard Strauss, Wagner and 16 other composers. 62 pieces. 343pp. 9 × 12. (Not available in France or Germany)
23447-9 Pa. **$19.95**

**RARE MASTERPIECES OF RUSSIAN PIANO MUSIC: Eleven Pieces by Glinka, Balakirev, Glazunov and Others, edited by Dmitry Feofanov.** Glinka's *Prayer,* Balakirev's *Reverie,* Liapunov's *Transcendental Etude, Op. 11, No. 10,* and eight others—full, authoritative scores from Russian texts. 144pp. 9 × 12.
24659-0 Pa. **$9.95**

**HUMORESQUES AND OTHER WORKS FOR SOLO PIANO, Antonín Dvořák.** Humoresques, Op. 101, complete, Silhouettes, Op. 8, Poetic Tone Pictures, Theme with Variations, Op. 36, 4 Slavonic Dances, more. 160pp. 9 × 12.
28355-0 Pa. **$10.95**

**PIANO MUSIC, Louis M. Gottschalk.** 26 pieces (including covers) by early 19th-century American genius. "Bamboula," "The Banjo," other Creole, Negro-based material, through elegant salon music. 301pp. 9⅛ × 12.
21683-7 Pa. **$15.95**

**SOUSA'S GREAT MARCHES IN PIANO TRANSCRIPTION, John Philip Sousa.** Playing edition includes: "The Stars and Stripes Forever," "King Cotton," "Washington Post," much more. 24 illustrations. 111pp. 9 × 12.
23132-1 Pa. **$7.95**

**COMPLETE PIANO RAGS, Scott Joplin.** All 38 piano rags by the acknowledged master of the form, reprinted from the publisher's original editions complete with sheet music covers. Introduction by David A. Jasen. 208pp. 9 × 12.
25807-6 Pa. **$9.95**

**RAGTIME REDISCOVERIES, selected by Trebor Jay Tichenor.** 64 unusual rags demonstrate diversity of style, local tradition. Original sheet music. 320pp. 9 × 12.
23776-1 Pa. **$14.95**

**RAGTIME RARITIES, edited by Trebor Jay Tichenor.** 63 tuneful, rediscovered piano rags by 51 composers (or teams). Does not duplicate selections in *Classic Piano Rags* (Dover, 20469-3). 305pp. 9 × 12.
23157-7 Pa. **$14.95**

**CLASSIC PIANO RAGS, selected with an introduction by Rudi Blesh.** Best ragtime music (1897–1922) by Scott Joplin, James Scott, Joseph F. Lamb, Tom Turpin, nine others. 364pp. 9 × 12.
20469-3 Pa. **$15.95**

**RAGTIME GEMS: Original Sheet Music for 25 Ragtime Classics, edited by David A. Jasen.** Includes original sheet music and covers for 25 rags, including three of Scott Joplin's finest: *Searchlight Rag, Rose Leaf Rag* and *Fig Leaf Rag.* 122pp. 9 × 12.
25248-5 Pa. **$8.95**

**NOCTURNES AND BARCAROLLES FOR SOLO PIANO, Gabriel Fauré.** 12 nocturnes and 12 barcarolles reprinted from authoritative French editions. 208pp. 9⅜ × 12¼. (Not available in France or Germany)
27955-3 Pa. **$12.95**

**FAVORITE WALTZES, POLKAS AND OTHER DANCES FOR SOLO PIANO, Johann Strauss, Jr.** Blue Danube, Tales from Vienna Woods, many other best-known waltzes and other dances. 160pp. 9 × 12.
27851-4 Pa. **$10.95**

**SELECTED PIANO WORKS FOR FOUR HANDS, Franz Schubert.** 24 separate pieces (16 most popular titles): Three Military Marches, Lebensstürme, Four Polonaises, Four Ländler, etc. Rehearsal numbers added. 273pp. 9 × 12.
23529-7 Pa. **$12.95**

*Available from your music dealer or write for **free** Music Catalog to Dover Publications, Inc., Dept. MUBI, 31 East 2nd Street, Mineola, N.Y. 11501.*

# *Dover Piano and Keyboard Editions*

**SHORTER WORKS FOR PIANOFORTE SOLO, Franz Schubert.** All piano music except Sonatas, Dances, and a few unfinished pieces. Contains Wanderer, Impromptus, Moments Musicals, Variations, Scherzi, etc. Breitkopf and Härtel edition. 199pp. 9⅜ × 12¼. 22648-4 Pa. **$11.95**

**WALTZES AND SCHERZOS, Frédéric Chopin.** All of the Scherzos and nearly all (20) of the Waltzes from the authoritative Mikuli edition. Editorial commentary. 160pp. 9 × 12. 24316-8 Pa. **$9.95**

**COMPLETE PRELUDES AND ETUDES FOR SOLO PIANO, Frédéric Chopin.** All 25 Preludes, all 27 Etudes by greatest composer of piano music. Authoritative Mikuli edition. 192pp. 9 × 12. 24052-5 Pa. **$8.95**

**COMPLETE BALLADES, IMPROMPTUS AND SONATAS, Frédéric Chopin.** The four Ballades, four Impromptus and three Sonatas. Authoritative Paderewski edition. 240pp. 9 × 12. (Available in U.S. only) 24164-5 Pa. **$10.95**

**NOCTURNES AND POLONAISES, Frédéric Chopin.** 20 *Nocturnes* and 11 *Polonaises* reproduced from the authoritative Mikuli edition for pianists, students, and musicologists. Commentary. 224pp. 9 × 12. 24564-0 Pa. **$10.95**

**COMPLETE MAZURKAS, Frédéric Chopin.** 51 best-loved compositions, reproduced directly from the authoritative Kistner edition edited by Carl Mikuli. 160pp. 9 × 12. 25548-4 Pa. **$8.95**

**FANTASY IN F MINOR, BARCAROLLE, BERCEUSE AND OTHER WORKS FOR SOLO PIANO, Frédéric Chopin.** 15 works, including one of the greatest of the Romantic period, the Fantasy in F Minor, Op. 49, reprinted from the authoritative German edition prepared by Chopin's student, Carl Mikuli. 224pp. 8⅜ × 11¼. 25950-1 Pa. **$7.95**

**COMPLETE HUNGARIAN RHAPSODIES FOR SOLO PIANO, Franz Liszt.** All 19 Rhapsodies reproduced directly from an authoritative Russian edition. All headings, footnotes translated to English. Best one volume edition available. 224pp. 8⅜ × 11¼. 24744-9 Pa. **$11.95**

**ANNÉES DE PÈLERINAGE, COMPLETE, Franz Liszt.** Authoritative Russian edition of piano masterpieces: *Première Année (Suisse): Deuxième Année (Italie)* and *Venezia e Napoli; Troisième Année,* other related pieces. 288pp. 9⅜ × 12¼. 25627-8 Pa. **$13.95**

**COMPLETE ETUDES FOR SOLO PIANO, Series I: Including the Transcendental Etudes, Franz Liszt, edited by Busoni.** Also includes Etude in 12 Exercises, 12 Grandes Etudes and Mazeppa. Breitkopf & Härtel edition. 272pp. 8⅜ × 11¼. 25815-7 Pa. **$12.95**

**COMPLETE ETUDES FOR SOLO PIANO, Series II: Including the Paganini Etudes and Concert Etudes, Franz Liszt, edited by Busoni.** Also includes Morceau de Salon, Ab Irato. Breitkopf & Härtel edition. 192pp. 8⅜ × 11¼. 25816-5 Pa. **$9.95**

**SONATA IN B MINOR AND OTHER WORKS FOR PIANO, Franz Liszt.** One of Liszt's most performed piano masterpieces, with the six Consolations, ten *Harmonies poetiques et religieuses,* two Ballades and two Legendes. Breitkopf & Härtel edition. 208pp. 8⅜ × 11¼. 26182-4 Pa. **$9.95**

**PIANO TRANSCRIPTIONS FROM FRENCH AND ITALIAN OPERAS, Franz Liszt.** Virtuoso transformations of themes by Mozart, Verdi, Bellini, other masters, into unforgettable music for piano. Published in association with American Liszt Society. 247pp. 9 × 12. 24273-0 Pa. **$13.95**

**MEPHISTO WALTZ AND OTHER WORKS FOR SOLO PIANO, Franz Liszt.** Rapsodie Espagnole, Liebestraüme Nos. 1–3, Valse Oubliée No. 1, Nuages Gris, Polonaises Nos. 1 and 2, Grand Galop Chromatique, more. 192pp. 8⅜ × 11¼. 28147-7 Pa. **$10.95**

**COMPLETE WORKS FOR PIANOFORTE SOLO, Felix Mendelssohn.** Breitkopf and Härtel edition of Capriccio in F# Minor, Sonata in E Major, Fantasy in F# Minor, Three Caprices, Songs without Words, and 20 other works. Total of 416pp. 9⅜ × 12¼. Two-vol. set. 23136-4, 23137-2 Pa. **$23.90**

**COMPLETE SONATAS AND VARIATIONS FOR SOLO PIANO, Johannes Brahms.** All sonatas, five variations on themes from Schumann, Paganini, Handel, etc. Vienna Gesellschaft der Musikfreunde edition. 178pp. 9 × 12. 22650-6 Pa. **$10.95**

**COMPLETE SHORTER WORKS FOR SOLO PIANO, Johannes Brahms.** All solo music not in other two volumes. Waltzes, Scherzo in E Flat Minor, Eight Pieces, Rhapsodies, Fantasies, Intermezzi, etc. Vienna Gesellschaft der Musikfreunde. 180pp. 9 × 12. 22651-4 Pa. **$10.95**

**COMPLETE TRANSCRIPTIONS, CADENZAS AND EXERCISES FOR SOLO PIANO, Johannes Brahms.** Vienna Gesellschaft der Musikfreunde edition, vol. 15. Studies after Chopin, Weber, Bach; gigues, sarabandes; 10 Hungarian dances, etc. 178pp. 9 × 12. 22652-2 Pa. **$10.95**

**PIANO MUSIC OF ROBERT SCHUMANN, Series I, edited by Clara Schumann.** Major compositions from the period 1830–39; *Papillons,* Toccata, Grosse Sonate No. 1, *Phantasiestücke, Arabeske, Blumenstück,* and nine other works. Reprinted from Breitkopf & Härtel edition. 274pp. 9⅜ × 12¼. 21459-1 Pa. **$13.95**

**PIANO MUSIC OF ROBERT SCHUMANN, Series II, edited by Clara Schumann.** Major compositions from period 1838–53; *Humoreske, Novelletten,* Sonate No. 2, 43 *Clavierstücke für die Jugend,* and six other works. Reprinted from Breitkopf & Härtel edition. 272pp. 9⅜ × 12¼. 21461-3 Pa. **$13.95**

**PIANO MUSIC OF ROBERT SCHUMANN, Series III, edited by Clara Schumann.** All solo music not in other two volumes, including *Symphonic Etudes, Phantaisie,* 13 other choice works. Definitive Breitkopf & Härtel edition. 224pp. 9⅜ × 12¼. 23906-3 Pa. **$11.95**

**PIANO MUSIC 1888–1905, Claude Debussy.** Deux Arabesques, Suite Bergamesque, Masques, first series of Images, etc. Nine others, in corrected editions. 175pp. 9⅜ × 12¼. 22771-5 Pa. **$8.95**

**COMPLETE PRELUDES, Books 1 and 2, Claude Debussy.** 24 evocative works that reveal the essence of Debussy's genius for musical imagery, among them many of the composer's most famous piano compositions. Glossary of French terms. 128pp. 8⅜ × 11¼. 25970-6 Pa. **$7.95**

**PRELUDES, BOOK I: The Autograph Score, Claude Debussy.** Superb facsimile reproduced directly from priceless autograph score in Pierpont Morgan Library in New York. New Introduction by Roy Howat. 48pp. 8⅛ × 11. 25549-2 Pa. **$8.95**

**PIANO MASTERPIECES OF MAURICE RAVEL, Maurice Ravel.** Handsome affordable treasury; *Pavane pour une infante defunte, jeux d'eau, Sonatine, Miroirs,* more. 128pp. 9 × 12. (Not available in France or Germany) 25137-3 Pa. **$8.95**

**COMPLETE LYRIC PIECES FOR PIANO, Edvard Grieg.** All 66 pieces from Grieg's ten sets of little mood pictures for piano, favorites of generations of pianists. 224pp. 9⅜ × 12¼. 26176-X Pa. **$11.95**

*Available from your music dealer or write for **free** Music Catalog to Dover Publications, Inc., Dept. MUBI, 31 East 2nd Street, Mineola, N.Y. 11501.*

# *Dover Orchestral Scores*

**THE SIX BRANDENBURG CONCERTOS AND THE FOUR ORCHESTRAL SUITES IN FULL SCORE, Johann Sebastian Bach.** Complete standard Bach-Gesellschaft editions in large, clear format. Study score. 273pp. 9 × 12. 23376-6 Pa. **$11.95**

**COMPLETE CONCERTI FOR SOLO KEYBOARD AND ORCHESTRA IN FULL SCORE, Johann Sebastian Bach.** Bach's seven complete concerti for solo keyboard and orchestra in full score from the authoritative Bach-Gesellschaft edition. 206pp. 9 × 12. 24929-8 Pa. **$11.95**

**THE THREE VIOLIN CONCERTI IN FULL SCORE, Johann Sebastian Bach.** Concerto in A Minor, BWV 1041; Concerto in E Major, BWV 1042; and Concerto for Two Violins in D Minor, BWV 1043. Bach-Gesellschaft editions. 64pp. 9⅜ × 12¼. 25124-1 Pa. **$6.95**

**GREAT ORGAN CONCERTI, OPP. 4 & 7, IN FULL SCORE, George Frideric Handel.** 12 organ concerti composed by great Baroque master are reproduced in full score from the *Deutsche Handelgesellschaft* edition. 138pp. 9⅜ × 12¼. 24462-8 Pa. **$8.95**

**COMPLETE CONCERTI GROSSI IN FULL SCORE, George Frideric Handel.** Monumental Opus 6 Concerti Grossi, Opus 3 and "Alexander's Feast" Concerti Grossi–19 in all–reproduced from most authoritative edition. 258pp. 9⅜ × 12¼. 24187-4 Pa. **$13.95**

**COMPLETE CONCERTI GROSSI IN FULL SCORE, Arcangelo Corelli.** All 12 concerti in the famous late nineteenth-century edition prepared by violinist Joseph Joachim and musicologist Friedrich Chrysander. 240pp. 8⅜ × 11¼. 25606-5 Pa. **$12.95**

**WATER MUSIC AND MUSIC FOR THE ROYAL FIREWORKS IN FULL SCORE, George Frideric Handel.** Full scores of two of the most popular Baroque orchestral works performed today–reprinted from definitive Deutsche Handelgesellschaft edition. Todal of 96pp. 8⅛ × 11. 25070-9 Pa. **$8.95**

**LATER SYMPHONIES, Wolfgang Amadeus Mozart.** Full orchestral scores to last symphonies (Nos. 35–41) reproduced from definitive Breitkopf & Härtel Complete Works edition. Study score. 285pp. 9 × 12. 23052-X Pa. **$12.95**

**17 DIVERTIMENTI FOR VARIOUS INSTRUMENTS, Wolfgang Amadeus Mozart.** Sparkling pieces of great vitality and brilliance from 1771–1779; consecutively numbered from 1 to 17. Reproduced from definitive Breitkopf & Härtel Complete Works edition. Study score. 241pp. 9⅜ × 12¼. 23862-8 Pa. **$13.95**

**PIANO CONCERTOS NOS. 11–16 IN FULL SCORE, Wolfgang Amadeus Mozart.** Authoritative Breitkopf & Härtel edition of six staples of the concerto repertoire, including Mozart's cadenzas for Nos. 12–16. 256pp. 9⅜ × 12¼. 25468-2 Pa. **$12.95**

**PIANO CONCERTOS NOS. 17–22, Wolfgang Amadeus Mozart.** Six complete piano concertos in full score, with Mozart's own cadenzas for Nos. 17–19. Breitkopf & Härtel edition. Study score. 370pp. 9⅜ × 12¼. 23599-8 Pa. **$16.95**

**PIANO CONCERTOS NOS. 23–27, Wolfgang Amadeus Mozart.** Mozart's last five piano concertos in full score, plus cadenzas for Nos. 23 and 27, and the Concert Rondo in D Major, K.382. Breitkopf & Härtel edition. Study score. 310pp. 9⅜ × 12¼. 23600-5 Pa. **$13.95**

**CONCERTI FOR WIND INSTRUMENTS IN FULL SCORE, Wolfgang Amadeus Mozart.** Exceptional volume contains ten pieces for orchestra and wind instruments and includes some of Mozart's finest, most popular music. 272pp. 9⅜ × 12¼. 25228-0 Pa. **$13.95**

**THE VIOLIN CONCERTI AND THE SINFONIA CONCERTANTE, K.364, IN FULL SCORE, Wolfgang Amadeus Mozart.** All five violin concerti and famed double concerto reproduced from authoritative Breitkopf & Härtel Complete Works Edition. 208pp. 9⅜ × 12¼. 25169-1 Pa. **$12.95**

**SYMPHONIES 88–92 IN FULL SCORE: The Haydn Society Edition, Joseph Haydn.** Full score of symphonies Nos. 88 through 92. Large, readable noteheads, ample margins for fingerings, etc., and extensive Editor's Commentary. 304pp. 9 × 12. (Available in U.S. only) 24445-8 Pa. **$15.95**

**THE MAGIC FLUTE (DIE ZAUBERFLÖTE) IN FULL SCORE, Wolfgang Amadeus Mozart.** Authoritative C. F. Peters edition of Mozart's last opera featuring all the spoken dialogue. Translation of German frontmatter. Dramatis personae. List of Numbers. 226pp. 9 × 12. 24783-X Pa. **$12.95**

**FOUR SYMPHONIES IN FULL SCORE, Franz Schubert.** Schubert's four most popular symphonies: No. 4 in C Minor ("Tragic"); No. 5 in B-flat Major; No. 8 in B Minor ("Unfinished"); and No. 9 in C Major ("Great"). Breitkopf & Härtel edition. Study score. 261pp. 9⅜ × 12¼. 23681-1 Pa. **$13.95**

**GREAT OVERTURES IN FULL SCORE, Carl Maria von Weber.** Overtures to *Oberon, Der Freischutz, Euryanthe* and *Preciosa* reprinted from authoritative Breitkopf & Härtel editions. 112pp. 9 × 12. 25225-6 Pa. **$9.95**

**SYMPHONIES NOS. 1, 2, 3, AND 4 IN FULL SCORE, Ludwig van Beethoven.** Republication of H. Litolff edition. 272pp. 9 × 12. 26033-X Pa. **$11.95**

**SYMPHONIES NOS. 5, 6 AND 7 IN FULL SCORE, Ludwig van Beethoven.** Republication of the H. Litolff edition. 272pp. 9 × 12. 26034-8 Pa. **$11.95**

**SYMPHONIES NOS. 8 AND 9 IN FULL SCORE, Ludwig van Beethoven.** Republication of the H. Litolff edition. 256pp. 9 × 12. 26035-6 Pa. **$11.95**

**SIX GREAT OVERTURES IN FULL SCORE, Ludwig van Beethoven.** Six staples of the orchestral repertoire from authoritative Breitkopf & Härtel edition. *Leonore Overtures,* Nos. 1–3; Overtures to *Coriolanus, Egmont, Fidelio.* 288pp. 9 × 12. 24789-9 Pa. **$13.95**

**COMPLETE PIANO CONCERTOS IN FULL SCORE, Ludwig van Beethoven.** Complete scores of five great Beethoven piano concertos, with all cadenzas as he wrote them, reproduced from authoritative Breitkopf & Härtel edition. New table of contents. 384pp. 9⅜ × 12¼. 24563-2 Pa. **$15.95**

**GREAT ROMANTIC VIOLIN CONCERTI IN FULL SCORE, Ludwig van Beethoven, Felix Mendelssohn and Peter Ilyitch Tchaikovsky.** The Beethoven Op. 61, Mendelssohn Op. 64 and Tchaikovsky Op. 35 concertos reprinted from the Breitkopf & Härtel editions. 224pp. 9 × 12. 24989-1 Pa. **$12.95**

**MAJOR ORCHESTRAL WORKS IN FULL SCORE, Felix Mendelssohn.** Generally considered to be Mendelssohn's finest orchestral works, here in one volume are: the complete *Midsummer Night's Dream; Hebrides Overture; Calm Sea and Prosperous Voyage Overture;* Symphony No. 3 in A ("Scottish"); and Symphony No. 4 in A ("Italian"). Breitkopf & Härtel edition. Study score. 406pp. 9 × 12. 23184-4 Pa. **$18.95**

**COMPLETE SYMPHONIES, Johannes Brahms.** Full orchestral scores. No. 1 in C Minor, Op. 68; No. 2 in D Major, Op. 73; No. 3 in F Major, Op. 90; and No. 4 in E Minor, Op. 98. Reproduced from definitive Vienna Gesellschaft der Musikfreunde edition. Study score. 344pp. 9 × 12. 23053-8 Pa. **$14.95**

*Available from your music dealer or write for* ***free*** *Music Catalog to Dover Publications, Inc., Dept. MUBI, 31 East 2nd Street, Mineola, N.Y. 11501.*

# Dover Orchestral Scores

**THREE ORCHESTRAL WORKS IN FULL SCORE: Academic Festival Overture, Tragic Overture and Variations on a Theme by Joseph Haydn, Johannes Brahms.** Reproduced from the authoritative Breitkopf & Härtel edition three of Brahms's great orchestral favorites. Editor's commentary in German and English. 112pp. 9⅜ × 12¼.
24637-X Pa. **$8.95**

**COMPLETE CONCERTI IN FULL SCORE, Johannes Brahms.** Piano Concertos Nos. 1 and 2; Violin Concerto, Op. 77; Concerto for Violin and Cello, Op. 102. Definitive Breitkopf & Härtel edition. 352pp. 9⅜ × 12¼.
24170-X Pa. **$16.95**

**COMPLETE SYMPHONIES IN FULL SCORE, Robert Schumann.** No. 1 in B-flat Major, Op. 38 ("Spring"); No. 2 in C Major, Op. 61; No. 3 in E flat Major, Op. 97 ("Rhenish"); and No. 4 in D Minor, Op. 120. Breitkopf & Härtel editions. Study score. 416pp. 9⅜ × 12¼. 24013-4 Pa. **$18.95**

**GREAT WORKS FOR PIANO AND ORCHESTRA IN FULL SCORE, Robert Schumann.** Collection of three superb pieces for piano and orchestra, including the popular Piano Concerto in A Minor. Breitkopf & Härtel edition. 183pp. 9⅜ × 12¼. 24340-0 Pa. **$10.95**

**THE PIANO CONCERTOS IN FULL SCORE, Frédéric Chopin.** The authoritative Breitkopf & Härtel full-score edition in one volume of Piano Concertos No. 1 in E Minor and No. 2 in F Minor. 176pp. 9 × 12.
25835-1 Pa. **$10.95**

**THE PIANO CONCERTI IN FULL SCORE, Franz Liszt.** Available in one volume the Piano Concerto No. 1 in E-flat Major and the Piano Concerto No. 2 in A Major—are among the most studied, recorded and performed of all works for piano and orchestra. 144pp. 9 × 12.
25221-3 Pa. **$8.95**

**SYMPHONY NO. 8 IN G MAJOR, OP. 88, SYMPHONY NO. 9 IN E MINOR, OP. 95 ("NEW WORLD") IN FULL SCORE, Antonín Dvořák.** Two celebrated symphonies by the great Czech composer, the Eighth and the immensely popular Ninth, "From the New World," in one volume. 272pp. 9 × 12. 24749-X Pa. **$13.95**

**FOUR ORCHESTRAL WORKS IN FULL SCORE: Rapsodie Espagnole, Mother Goose Suite, Valses Nobles et Sentimentales, and Pavane for a Dead Princess, Maurice Ravel.** Four of Ravel's most popular orchestral works, reprinted from original full-score French editions. 240pp. 9⅜ × 12¼. (Not available in France or Germany)
25962-5 Pa. **$13.95**

**DAPHNIS AND CHLOE IN FULL SCORE, Maurice Ravel.** Definitive full-score edition of Ravel's rich musical setting of a Greek fable by Longus is reprinted here from the original French edition. 320pp. 9⅜ × 12¼. (Not available in France or Germany)
25826-2 Pa. **$15.95**

**THREE GREAT ORCHESTRAL WORKS IN FULL SCORE, Claude Debussy.** Three favorites by influential modernist: *Prélude à l'Après-midi d'un Faune, Nocturnes,* and *La Mer.* Reprinted from early French editions. 279pp. 9 × 12. 24441-5 Pa. **$13.95**

**SYMPHONY IN D MINOR IN FULL SCORE, César Franck.** Superb, authoritative edition of Franck's only symphony, an often-performed and recorded masterwork of late French romantic style. 160pp. 9 × 12.
25373-2 Pa. **$9.95**

**THE GREAT WALTZES IN FULL SCORE, Johann Strauss, Jr.** Complete scores of eight melodic masterpieces: The Beautiful Blue Danube, Emperor Waltz, Tales of the Vienna Woods, Wiener Blut, four more. Authoritative editions. 336pp. 8⅜ × 11¼. 26009-7 Pa. **$14.95**

**FOURTH, FIFTH AND SIXTH SYMPHONIES IN FULL SCORE, Peter Ilyitch Tchaikovsky.** Complete orchestral scores of Symphony No. 4 in F Minor, Op. 36; Symphony No. 5 in E Minor, Op. 64; Symphony No. 6 in B Minor, "Pathetique," Op. 74. Study score. Breitkopf & Härtel editions. 480pp. 9⅜ × 12¼. 23861-X Pa. **$19.95**

**ROMEO AND JULIET OVERTURE AND CAPRICCIO ITALIEN IN FULL SCORE, Peter Ilyitch Tchaikovsky.** Two of Russian master's most popular compositions in high quality, inexpensive reproduction. From authoritative Russian edition. 208pp. 8⅜ × 11½. 25217-5 Pa. **$10.95**

**NUTCRACKER SUITE IN FULL SCORE, Peter Ilyitch Tchaikovsky.** Among the most popular ballet pieces ever created—a complete, inexpensive, high-quality score to study and enjoy. 128pp. 9 × 12.
25379-1 Pa. **$9.95**

**TONE POEMS, SERIES I: DON JUAN, TOD UND VERKLARUNG, and DON QUIXOTE, Richard Strauss.** Three of the most often performed and recorded works in entire orchestral repertoire, reproduced in full score from original editions. Study score. 286pp. 9⅜ × 12¼. (Available in U.S. only)
23754-0 Pa. **$14.95**

**TONE POEMS, SERIES II: TILL EULENSPIEGELS LUSTIGE STREICHE, ALSO SPRACH ZARATHUSTRA, and EIN HELDEN-LEBEN, Richard Strauss.** Three important orchestral works, including very popular *Till Eulenspiegel's Merry Pranks,* reproduced in full score from original editions. Study score. 315pp. 9⅜ × 12¼. (Available in U.S. only)
23755-9 Pa. **$14.95**

**DAS LIED VON DER ERDE IN FULL SCORE, Gustav Mahler.** Mahler's masterpiece, a fusion of song and symphony, reprinted from the original 1912 Universal Edition. English translations of song texts. 160pp. 9 × 12. 25657-X Pa. **$9.95**

**SYMPHONIES NOS. 1 AND 2 IN FULL SCORE, Gustav Mahler.** Unabridged, authoritative Austrian editions of Symphony No. 1 in D Major ("Titan") and Symphony No. 2 in C Minor ("Resurrection"). 384pp. 8⅛ × 11. 25473-9 Pa. **$14.95**

**SYMPHONIES NOS. 3 AND 4 IN FULL SCORE, Gustav Mahler.** Two brilliantly contrasting masterworks—one scored for a massive ensemble, the other for small orchestra and soloist—reprinted from authoritative Viennese editions. 368pp. 9⅜ × 12¼. 26166-2 Pa. **$16.95**

**SYMPHONY NO. 8 IN FULL SCORE, Gustav Mahler.** Superb authoritative edition of massive, complex "Symphony of a Thousand." Scored for orchestra, eight solo voices, double chorus, boys' choir and organ. Reprint of Izdatel'stvo "Muzyka," Moscow, edition. Translation of texts. 272pp. 9⅜ × 12¼. 26022-4 Pa. **$12.95**

**THE FIREBIRD IN FULL SCORE (Original 1910 Version), Igor Stravinsky.** Handsome, inexpensive edition of modern masterpiece, renowned for brilliant orchestration, glowing color. Authoritative Russian edition. 176pp. 9⅜ × 12¼. (Available in U.S. only) 25535-2 Pa. **$10.95**

**PETRUSHKA IN FULL SCORE: Original Version, Igor Stravinsky.** The definitive full-score edition of Stravinsky's masterful score for the great Ballets Russes 1911 production of *Petrushka.* 160pp. 9⅜ × 12¼. (Available in U.S. only) 25680-4 Pa. **$11.95**

**THE RITE OF SPRING IN FULL SCORE, Igor Stravinsky.** A reprint of the original full-score edition of the most famous musical work of the 20th century, created as a ballet score for Diaghilev's Ballets Russes. 176pp. 9⅜ × 12¼. (Available in U.S. only) 25857-2 Pa. **$9.95**

*Available from your music dealer or write for **free** Music Catalog to*
*Dover Publications, Inc., Dept. MUBI, 31 East 2nd Street, Mineola, N.Y. 11501.*

# Dover Chamber Music Scores

COMPLETE SUITES FOR UNACCOMPANIED CELLO AND SONATAS FOR VIOLA DA GAMBA, Johann Sebastian Bach. Bach-Gesellschaft edition of the six cello suites (BWV 1007–1012) and three sonatas (BWV 1027–1029), commonly played today on the cello. 112pp. 9⅜ × 12¼. 25641-3 Pa. **$8.95**

WORKS FOR VIOLIN, Johann Sebastian Bach. Complete Sonatas and Partitas for Unaccompanied Violin; Six Sonatas for Violin and Clavier. Bach-Gesellschaft edition. 158pp. 9⅜ × 12¼. 23683-8 Pa. **$9.95**

COMPLETE STRING QUARTETS, Wolfgang Amadeus Mozart. Breitkopf & Härtel edition. All 23 string quartets plus alternate slow movement to K.156. Study score. 277pp. 9⅜ × 12¼. 22372-8 Pa. **$13.95**

COMPLETE STRING QUINTETS, Wolfgang Amadeus Mozart. All the standard-instrumentation string quintets, plus String Quintet in C Minor, K.406; Quintet with Horn or Second Cello, K.407; and Clarinet Quintet, K.581. Breitkopf & Härtel edition. Study score. 181pp. 9⅜ × 12¼. 23603-X Pa. **$9.95**

STRING QUARTETS, OPP. 20 and 33, COMPLETE, Joseph Haydn. Complete reproductions of the 12 masterful quartets (six each) of Opp. 20 and 33–in the reliable Eulenburg edition. 272pp. 8⅜ × 11¼. 24852-6 Pa. **$12.95**

STRING QUARTETS, OPP. 42, 50 and 54, Joseph Haydn. Complete reproductions of Op. 42 in D Minor; Op. 50, Nos. 1–6 ("Prussian Quartets") and Op. 54, Nos. 1–3. Reliable Eulenburg edition. 224pp. 8⅜ × 11¼. 24262-5 Pa. **$12.95**

TWELVE STRING QUARTETS, Joseph Haydn. 12 often-performed works: Op. 55, Nos. 1–3 (including *Razor*); Op. 64, Nos. 1–6; Op. 71, Nos. 1–3. Definitive Eulenburg edition. 288pp. 8⅜ × 11¼. 23933-0 Pa. **$13.95**

ELEVEN LATE STRING QUARTETS, Joseph Haydn. Complete reproductions of Op. 74, Nos. 1–3; Op. 76, Nos. 1–6; and Op. 77, Nos. 1 and 2. Definitive Eulenburg edition. Full-size study score. 320pp. 8⅜ × 11¼. 23753-2 Pa. **$13.95**

COMPLETE STRING QUARTETS, Ludwig van Beethoven. Breitkopf & Härtel edition. Six quartets of Opus 18; three quartets of Opus 59; Opera 74, 95, 127, 130, 131, 132, 135 and Grosse Fuge. Study score. 434pp. 9⅜ × 12¼. 22361-2 Pa. **$16.95**

SIX GREAT PIANO TRIOS IN FULL SCORE, Ludwig van Beethoven. Definitive Breitkopf & Härtel edition of Beethoven's Piano Trios Nos. 1–6 including the "Ghost" and the "Archduke." 224pp. 9⅜ × 12¼. 25398-8 Pa. **$11.95**

COMPLETE VIOLIN SONATAS, Ludwig van Beethoven. All ten sonatas including the "Kreutzer" and "Spring" sonatas in the definitive Breitkopf & Härtel edition. 256pp. 9 × 12. 26277-4 Pa. **$13.95**

COMPLETE SONATAS AND VARIATIONS FOR CELLO AND PIANO, Ludwig van Beethoven. All five sonatas and three sets of variations. Reprinted from Breitkopf & Härtel edition. 176pp. 9⅜ × 12¼. 26441-6 Pa. **$10.95**

COMPLETE CHAMBER MUSIC FOR STRINGS, Franz Schubert. Reproduced from famous Breitkopf & Härtel edition: Quintet in C Major (1828), 15 quartets and two trios for violin(s), viola, and violincello. Study score. 348pp. 9 × 12. 21463-X Pa. **$15.95**

CAPRICE VIENNOIS AND OTHER FAVORITE PIECES FOR VIOLIN AND PIANO: With Separate Violin Part, Fritz Kreisler. *Liebesfreud, Liebesleid, Schön Rosmarin, Sicilienne and Rigaudon,* more. 64pp. plus slip-in violin part. 9 × 12. (Available in U.S. only) 28489-1 Pa. **$7.95**

COMPLETE CHAMBER MUSIC FOR PIANOFORTE AND STRINGS, Franz Schubert. Breitkopf & Härtel edition. *Trout,* Quartet in F Major, and trios for piano, violin, cello. Study score. 192pp. 9 × 12. 21527-X Pa. **$11.95**

CHAMBER WORKS FOR PIANO AND STRINGS, Felix Mendelssohn. Eleven of the composer's best known works in the genre–duos, trios, quartets and a sextet–reprinted from authoritative Breitkopf & Härtel edition. 384pp. 9⅜ × 12¼. 26117-4 Pa. **$19.95**

COMPLETE CHAMBER MUSIC FOR STRINGS, Felix Mendelssohn. All of Mendelssohn's chamber music: Octet, Two Quintets, Six Quartets, and Four Pieces for String Quartet. (Nothing with piano is included.) Complete works edition (1874–7). Study score. 283pp. 9⅜ × 12¼. 23679-X Pa. **$13.95**

CHAMBER MUSIC OF ROBERT SCHUMANN, edited by Clara Schumann. Superb collection of three trios, four quartets, and piano quintet. Breitkopf & Härtel edition. 288pp. 9⅜ × 12¼. 24101-7 Pa. **$14.95**

COMPLETE SONATAS FOR SOLO INSTRUMENT AND PIANO, Johannes Brahms. All seven sonatas–three for violin, two for cello and two for clarinet (or viola)–reprinted from the authoritative Breitkopf & Härtel edition. 208pp. 9 × 12. 26091-7 Pa. **$12.95**

COMPLETE CHAMBER MUSIC FOR STRINGS AND CLARINET QUINTET, Johannes Brahms. Vienna Gesellschaft der Musikfreunde edition of all quartets, quintets, and sextet without piano. Study edition. 262pp. 8⅜ × 11¼. 21914-3 Pa. **$12.95**

QUINTET AND QUARTETS FOR PIANO AND STRINGS, Johannes Brahms. Full scores of *Quintet in F Minor,* Op. 34; *Quartet in G Minor,* Op. 25; *Quartet in A Major,* Op. 26; *Quartet in C Minor,* Op. 60. Breitkopf & Härtel edition. 298pp. 9 × 12. 24900-X Pa. **$15.95**

COMPLETE PIANO TRIOS, Johannes Brahms. All five piano trios in the definitive Breitkopf & Härtel edition. 288pp. 9 × 12. 25769-X Pa. **$14.95**

CHAMBER WORKS FOR PIANO AND STRINGS, Antonín Dvořák. Society editions of the F Minor and Dumky piano trios, D Major and E-flat Major piano quartets and A Major piano quintet. 352pp. 8⅜ × 11¼. (Available in U.S. only) 25663-4 Pa. **$15.95**

FIVE LATE STRING QUARTETS, Antonín Dvořák. Treasury of Czech master's finest chamber works: Nos. 10, 11, 12, 13, 14. Reliable Simrock editions. 282pp. 8¼ × 11. 25135-7 Pa. **$12.95**

STRING QUARTETS BY DEBUSSY AND RAVEL/Claude Debussy: Quartet in G Minor, Op. 10/Maurice Ravel: Quartet in F Major, Claude Debussy and Maurice Ravel. Authoritative one-volume edition of two influential masterpieces noted for individuality, delicate and subtle beauties. 112pp. 8⅜ × 11. (Not available in France or Germany) 25231-0 Pa. **$7.95**

GREAT CHAMBER WORKS, César Franck. Four great works: Violin Sonata in A Major, Piano Trio in F-sharp Minor, String Quartet in D Major and Piano Quintet in F Minor. From J. Hamelle, Paris and C. F. Peters, Leipzig editions. 248pp. 9⅜ × 12¼. 26546-3 Pa. **$13.95**

COMPLETE STRING QUARTETS, Peter Ilyitch Tchaikovsky and Alexander Borodin. Tchaikovsky's Quartets Nos. 1–3 and Borodin's Quartets Nos. 1 and 2 reproduced from authoritative editions. 240pp. 8⅜ × 11¼. 28333-X Pa. **$12.95**